PROBLEM PLAYS

ANN FARQUHAR-SMITH

HULTON EDUCATIONAL
PUBLICATIONS

© 1977
Ann Farquhar-Smith

ISBN 0 7175 0778 5

By the same author:
EIGHT PLAYS TO FINISH
MORE PLAYS TO FINISH

First published 1977 by Hulton Educational Publications Ltd.,
Raans Road, Amersham, Bucks.
Filmset in "Monophoto" Times 11 on 13 pt. and
printed in Great Britain by
Fletcher & Son Ltd., Norwich

INTRODUCTION

Problems confront us all through our lives—in school, in the family, at work, in our leisure. Many people think that there is always some kind of benevolent brother in the form of a welfare state to take care of them. Problems are not for them to bother about. But in fact problems have to be lived with—and solved—by each of us personally.

As you take part in these plays you will realise that participation in the problem situations means understanding other people's points of view, trying to think out solutions yourself and looking broadly at the kind of society we live in.

The discussion questions which follow each play will help you to explore these problems.

CONTENTS

FRIENDS AND NEIGHBOURS

★

Characters

MOHINDER SINGH SANDHU, *Father*
AMARJIT KAUR SANDHU, *Mother*
RAVINDER SINGH SANDHU, *Son*
PIARA KAUR SANDHU, *Daughter*
KEN CALDER, *Father*
FREDA CALDER, *Mother*
BRENDA CALDER, *Daughter*
STEVE CALDER, *Son*

Friends and Neighbours

Scene I

The Calders' house

BRENDA: Come quick, Mum! Look who's moving into the Gordons' house!

MRS. CALDER: They've sold it at last, have they? I'm amazed that they found a buyer for it—the state it was in.

BRENDA: But come and see who's bought it!

STEVE: Is it someone we know?

BRENDA: It's someone that Mum isn't going to want to know.

MR. CALDER: How can you tell that just by looking at them?

BRENDA: You come and look at them and you'll see what I mean. They're Sikhs!

MRS. CALDER: They're what?

BRENDA: Sikhs. Indians from the Punjab. They wear turbans—at least the men do.

MR. CALDER: Indians living in this street!

MRS. CALDER: You're right, Brenda. The man's got a turban.

BRENDA: So has the boy. The Sikhs have to keep their hair covered.

MR. CALDER: How do you know so much about it?

BRENDA: We've done it in R.I. at school. They never cut their hair either.

MRS. CALDER: Or wash it, I suppose.

MR. CALDER: Look at the way that woman's dressed. Quite unsuitable for our climate.

MRS. CALDER: Ken, I've been telling you for months that this neighbourhood has been going downhill. Now it's hit rock bottom. We'll never be able to open our windows for the smell of curry. Oh Ken, can't you do something about it? Complain to somebody?

MR. CALDER: They're the only ones who could do any complaining. We haven't got a leg to stand on. I'd be in trouble if I complained about them.

STEVE: They'll be coming to our school I expect. I wonder if their kid plays football.

MRS. CALDER: Don't you talk like that. I'm not having a child of mine making friends with those blacks!

BRENDA: They're not black, Mum, more coffee coloured.

MR. CALDER: What does that matter? They're not English and they're not white.

STEVE: So what? Who says everyone has to be white and English?

MRS. CALDER: Don't you talk to your father like that. This is our country and we don't want it overrun by a bunch of foreigners who can't find work in their own country.

MR. CALDER: They all come here to live off the dole.

STEVE: They'll need a bit more than dole money to live in that house.

MRS. CALDER: Just you wait. They won't be the only ones living in that house. Another few weeks and they'll have another three families in there with them.

BRENDA: We'll just have to wait and see, won't we?

Scene II

The Sandhus' house. A few weeks later.

MR. SANDHU: Well, how do you like your new house?

MRS. SANDHU: I like the house, but I don't think the neighbours are very friendly.

RAVINDER: The boy across the road talked to me at school today. He seems quite friendly. He plays inside left.

MR. SANDHU: You and your football. A boy of your age should have other things on his mind. You could start helping me with the car.

PIARA: The girl from across the road seems quite nice too. She asked me how we liked it here.

MR. SANDHU: That's all right. But you keep your friendship only with the *girl* across the road.

MRS. SANDHU: It's bad enough having you go to the same school as boys. We don't want to start having friendships with boys as well. And certainly not white boys. What would your grandmother say?

PIARA: You remind me about that every day, Mother. I'm not likely to forget. And if grandmother could only see the spotty youths we have in our class, she wouldn't worry.

MRS. SANDHU: Listen to how she talks to me. She wouldn't dare talk to me like that in the old country.

RAVINDER: But we're not living in the old country any more. We're living in England and we should try to adapt.

MRS. SANDHU: Why should we adapt? Our ways are better. They're a bunch of short-haired barbarians. They let their girls do as they please. They haven't a sense of honour within the family as we have. They have no religion and no principles.

MR. SANDHU: But we've chosen to live among them, so we can at least try to put up with them, can't we?

MRS. SANDHU: I'll try to put up with them, but I'll never approve of them.

(*Sudden crash.*)

MR. SANDHU: What was that?

RAVINDER: It sounded like breaking glass.

PIARA: It came from the kitchen.

RAVINDER: I'll go and see what it was.

(*Goes out.*)

MR. SANDHU: I told you not to put too many glasses in that cupboard. I warned you it would fall down if you did.

MRS. SANDHU: I didn't put too many glasses in that cupboard. If it's fallen down, it's because you didn't put the cupboard up correctly in the first place.

RAVINDER: (*Comes in.*) Look what someone's just thrown through the kitchen window!

MR. SANDHU: It's a brick.

PIARA: There's a piece of paper wrapped round it.

MRS. SANDHU: What does it say? That looks like English writing.

RAVINDER: It says, "Go home you black . . ." I'd better not say the next word.

MRS. SANDHU: So this is the sort of thing English people get up to? Break our windows with bricks and tell us to go home! We've bought our house like anyone else. We've a right to live where we choose.

MR. SANDHU: Someone doesn't agree with you. Did you see anyone, Ravinder?

RAVINDER: No. The back garden was empty.

PIARA: What should we do now? Phone the police?

MR. SANDHU: I don't want to bother them with this. They've got enough to do around here. We're not hurt.

MRS. SANDHU: Only the window and our feelings have been

hurt. You'd better get that window mended as soon as possible. The kitchen is cold enough.

MR. SANDHU: I'll go and fix it right away until I can get a new piece of glass tomorrow. Come on, Ravinder, you can give me a hand.

Scene III

The Calders' house. A few days later.

STEVE: Dad! Mum! Have you heard what's happened to the Sandhus?

MRS. CALDER: They've moved?

STEVE: No, Mum. Someone chucked a brick through their kitchen window.

MRS. CALDER: That's awful. Was anyone hurt?

STEVE: No. Luckily they were in the front room at the time.

MR. CALDER: Who would want to do a thing like that?

BRENDA: From the way you've been going on about the Sandhus I wouldn't be a bit surprised to hear that you'd done it.

MR. CALDER: How dare you talk like that? We may not approve of blacks living in our street, but we don't mean them any harm.

MRS. CALDER: Have they told the police?

STEVE: Ravinder says that the police have enough to do, without troubling them with this small incident.

MR. CALDER: He must be a very tolerant man. If someone chucked a brick through my window, I wouldn't rest until I'd found out who did it.

MRS. CALDER: He may be tolerant, but he's not very quiet. He's revving up that engine again. Gets on your nerves, doesn't it?

MR. CALDER: Oh Freda, stop complaining. He's a mechanic by trade. He works down at McAdam's garage. I was thinking of asking him to have a look at our car. I've got something wrong with the ignition.

MRS. CALDER: Ken Calder, it's bad enough that the children have made friends with these black kids. They can't really help it, going to the same school and that. But I forbid you to go and ask that man for help. What would the neighbours say?

MR. CALDER: With the labour charges at the garage what they are today, I don't care what the neighbours say. But just to please you, I'll take it to McAdam's and pay £20 for our Sikh neighbour to fix it.

(*Knock at the door.*)

STEVE: I'll go. It'll probably be Ravinder.

(*Steve goes out.*)

BRENDA: Piara said she might come over as well.

MRS. CALDER: I wish you would tell the kids not to be so friendly with those Sikhs.

MR. CALDER: Frightened of what the neighbours might say, are you, Freda?

(*Ravinder, Piara and Steve come in.*)

MRS. CALDER: Hello, Ravinder and Piara.

RAVINDER: Good afternoon, Mrs. Calder. How are you?

MRS. CALDER: Very well, thank you, Ravinder.

STEVE: We're going upstairs. I want Ravinder to help me with my model.

MR. CALDER: Be careful with that new modelling knife you bought this morning. It's a lot sharper than your old one.

BRENDA: Piara's coming up to my room to listen to records.

MRS. CALDER: Well, mind you don't go playing them too loud.

PIARA: No, Mrs. Calder, I'll make sure that we don't disturb you.

(*Ravinder, Piara, Steve and Brenda go out.*)

MRS. CALDER: I must give credit where credit is due. Those kids have got lovely manners.

MR. CALDER: Better than our two?

MRS. CALDER: I hate to say it, Ken, but yes they are.

MR. CALDER: They are brought up to respect their elders. I think our two could do with a bit of that.

MRS. CALDER: I'm not sure that all this modern freedom is good for kids.

MR. CALDER: Don't you worry, Freda. There's not much wrong with our two.

(*Ravinder and Steve come in.*)

RAVINDER: Mrs. Calder. Come quick. Steve has cut his thumb.

MR. CALDER: I warned you about that knife.

STEVE: It slipped, Dad. I couldn't help it.

MRS. CALDER: Stop yelling at the boy and do something.

MR. CALDER: There's nothing much we can do. He'll have to go to hospital with this. Get some cotton-wool, Freda, to stop the bleeding.

MRS. CALDER: Here you are. You're going to need the whole packet.

MR. CALDER: Get your coat on, Freda, and come on.

MRS. CALDER: Oh no, Ken. You take him. You know how I feel about hospitals. I'll faint or do something silly.

MR. CALDER: All right. Suit yourself. Come on you two.

MRS. CALDER: You're not taking Ravinder?

MR. CALDER: Why not? He can keep Steve company.

(*Mr. Calder, Steve and Ravinder go out.*)

MRS. CALDER: Oh dear, I feel a bit faint. I'll have to sit down.

(*Piara and Brenda come in.*)

BRENDA: What's going on, Mum? You look a bit white and peaky.

MRS. CALDER: Our Steve's taken the top off his thumb with that new modelling knife. Dad's taking him to hospital.

PIARA: That's awful, Mrs. Calder. I hope he'll be all right.

MRS. CALDER: Ravinder's gone with them. You'd better go and tell your parents what's happened, Piara, in case they're late back.

PIARA: Of course, Mrs. Calder. I'll go over now. (*Goes out.*)

BRENDA: How bad is it, Mum?

MRS. CALDER: Pretty bad, Brenda. The top of his thumb's hanging off. But if they can get to hospital quickly enough, I'm sure they'll be able to fix it.

(*Mr. Calder comes in.*)

MRS. CALDER: Ken! What are you doing here?

MR. CALDER: The flaming car won't start. Dead as a door-nail.

MRS. CALDER: Ring for an ambulance, then.

MR. CALDER: That's what I've come in for. (*Picks up phone.*) 9 – 9 – 9. Hello. Yes please. Ambulance please. Hello. Yes, my son's had a bit of an accident. Oh yes. The top of his thumb. No. My car won't start. What! But he's got to get to hospital. All right. (*Puts phone down.*)

MRS. CALDER: What's wrong, Ken?

MR. CALDER: There's been a pile-up on the motorway and

they won't be able to send an ambulance for at least half an hour.

MRS. CALDER: Try Mr. Aitken next door.

MR. CALDER: Right. 3 – 4 – 7 – 2 – 1. Hello, Frank. It's Ken here. Look, we've got a bit of a problem. Steve's taken the top off his thumb with a knife. My car won't start so I can't get him to hospital. Can you take him in your car? Bleeding? Yes, of course, it's bleeding. You've just cleaned your car. O.K. Forget it. Sorry I asked.

MRS. CALDER: Won't he do it, then?

MR. CALDER: He's just cleaned out the inside of his car and he doesn't want blood all over it.

MRS. CALDER: What are we going to do now, Ken?

(*Mr. and Mrs. Sandhu come in with Piara.*)

MR. SANDHU: I hope you don't mind us coming in like this, but the front door was wide open.

MR. CALDER: That's all right, Mr. Sandhu.

MR. SANDHU: I hear you've got a problem. Can we help in any way?

MR. CALDER: Steve's chopped the top off his thumb. My car won't start, so we can't get him to hospital.

MR. SANDHU: What are we waiting for? My car's just across the road, and it's in tip-top condition.

MR. CALDER: Thanks very much. Let's go now. I left the boys waiting in my car.

(*Mr. Calder and Mr. Sandhu go out.*)

MRS. SANDHU: Mrs. Calder, you look exhausted. Let me make you a cup of tea.

MRS. CALDER: Do you drink tea, then?

MRS. SANDHU: Of course we do. Where do you think tea comes from?

MRS. CALDER: Oh, how silly of me. I'd love a cup of tea.

MRS. SANDHU: Come on, Piara. Help me make a cup of tea for Mrs. Calder.

(*Piara and Mrs. Sandhu go out.*)

BRENDA: Oh dear, Mum. What will the neighbours say?

MRS. CALDER: As far as I'm concerned they can say what they like. A friend in need is a friend indeed and I couldn't care less what colour they are.

FRIENDS AND NEIGHBOURS

Points to Discuss

1. Do you think that immigration should be stopped? If so, why?

2. Why do you think that some white people are prejudiced against people of other colours?

3. Do you think that all people are created equal—regardless of colour, race or religion?

4. Has the native British way of life been changed by large numbers of immigrants? If so, how? Should Britain have an "open door" policy and allow in as many people of other races as wish to settle here? Give reasons.

5. Discuss the problems that British people may meet if they in turn become immigrants—in Canada or Australia, for instance.

Things to Do

1. Find out about the Asian people living in or near your area. How many come from India, how many from Pakistan? What are their religions? What languages do they speak? Have any arrived from East Africa? If so, how did they come to live there?

2. What would happen if all the immigrants left? Where do the immigrants work? In what ways do immigrant people help the community?

3. Look at your prejudices. Are they *your* prejudices? Have you reasons for them? Or have your prejudices

been influenced by what your parents and teachers think?

4. Find out about the religion of the Sikhs, the Hindus and the Moslems. In what ways are they different from or similar to Christianity?

JUST THE JOB

★

Characters

MR. CARTER, *Personnel Manager of Exton's*
MISS POMEROY, *his secretary*
CLIVE RAWLINS, *applicant for a job at Exton's*
MR. RAWLINS, *Clive's father*
MRS. RAWLINS, *Clive's mother*
TOBY SKINNER, *another applicant for a job at Exton's*
JULIE ROSS, *Toby's girlfriend*

Just the Job

Scene I

Mr. Carter's office

MR. CARTER: I've narrowed it down to these two, Miss Pomeroy. Some of these letters are a disgrace. A sad reflection on our educational system.

MISS POMEROY: Spelling seems to have gone right out of fashion.

MR. CARTER: And so does handwriting. Doesn't anyone show them how to set out a letter any more? You'd think they'd make a bit of an effort when they're applying for a job.

MISS POMEROY: Have you seen this one? "Dear Sir, I want a job with your firm. My mum says I'm good with my hands. I ain't got no exams at school."

MR. CARTER: How they think they can do a day's work for us when they haven't worked at school is quite beyond me. Anyway, these two seem to be the best of a bad lot: Clive Rawlins and Toby Skinner. Quite good letters, and this one, Skinner, even mentions his hobbies.

MISS POMEROY: I don't see what that's got to do with getting a job as a fitter.

MR. CARTER: It shows that the lad's interested in something else besides girls and pop music. Make appointments for me to see them some time soon. Next Tuesday afternoon would do very well, I think. I'm free all that day.

Scene II

The Rawlins' house

CLIVE: Mum! I've got an appointment for an interview with the Personnel Manager at Exton's on Tuesday.

MRS. RAWLINS: Well done, Clive. An interview means you've nearly got the job.

MR. RAWLINS: But he hasn't yet, has he?

MRS. RAWLINS: Appearance is most important at an interview, dear. You'd better think about what you're going to wear.

MR. RAWLINS: Your mother's right. You'll need to wear a suit.

CLIVE: But I haven't got a suit.

MRS. RAWLINS: Yes you have. There's the one you wore to your Auntie Vi's wedding.

CLIVE: That won't fit me. I've grown a bit since then.

MRS. RAWLINS: I can let it out. You've not grown that much.

MR. RAWLINS: And you'll have to get your hair cut.

CLIVE: What on earth for? I'm not joining the Army. I want a job as a fitter.

MRS. RAWLINS: Do as your father says, dear. First impressions are important. You've let your hair get a bit out of hand since you left school.

CLIVE: I like it like this.

MR. RAWLINS: You may like it like that, but the Personnel Manager won't.

CLIVE: I'd rather draw the dole than have a short back and sides.

MR. RAWLINS: You can let it grow again after the interview.

CLIVE: I'm not applying to be managing director, you know. Have I got to go to all this trouble?

MR. RAWLINS: With jobs as scarce as they are nowadays, nothing's too much trouble.

CLIVE: And nothing is what I'd like to do!

Scene III

Toby Skinner's house

JULIE: That's great, Toby. An interview with the Personnel Manager. That's almost as good as getting a job.

TOBY: But it isn't the same as getting a job. There's bound to be other blokes there being interviewed.

JULIE: You've got to go in there and convince the man that you will do the job better than anyone else.

TOBY: How do I do that?

JULIE: Be enthusiastic. Try and guess what answers he wants to his questions. If someone is going to pay you money for working, you've got to make them think that you'll give them their money's worth.

TOBY: That makes sense. I'll try. I've been for interviews before and somehow I don't seem to have got over to the bloke what I wanted to say.

JULIE: You need to project yourself. Anyway, our Miss Imrie says that the secret of the interview is how you look.

TOBY: Does that mean I've got to have my hair cut?

JULIE: Not really. But make sure it's tidy. I'll do it for you the night before.

TOBY: What'll I wear then? I can't get into my school blazer any more.

JULIE: Anything will do, as long as it's not too way out, and it's neat and tidy.

TOBY: T-shirt and jeans?

JULIE: That's too way out. Your new jacket's nice—it'll do. I'll press it for you, and a pair of trousers.

TOBY: I'm glad I asked your advice.

JULIE: And don't forget. Be on time. Play it safe and be a bit early. Nobody's going to give a job to someone who can't turn up for an interview on time.

TOBY: Well, if 1 do get the job—it'll all be thanks to you.

Scene IV

Mr. Carter's office

MR. CARTER: Miss Pomeroy, will you send in Mr. Rawlins please.

MISS POMEROY: I'm sorry, Mr. Carter, but Mr. Rawlins hasn't turned up yet.

MR. CARTER: That's a good start. What about the other one—Skinner. Is he here yet?

MISS POMEROY: Yes, he's here. I'll send him in now.

(*Miss Pomeroy goes out and Toby comes in.*)

MR. CARTER: Good afternoon. Toby Skinner, isn't it?

TOBY: Yes, sir.

MR. CARTER: You don't mind if I call you Toby, do you? Do sit down. That chair over there.

TOBY: Thank you.

MR. CARTER: You're very early, aren't you?

TOBY: Yes, sir. It was my girlfriend's idea. She said that if I didn't have anything better to do, I should make a point of getting here in good time.

MR. CARTER: She sounds a very sensible young lady.

TOBY: She is, sir.

MR. CARTER: I see from your application form that you went to Grange Modern School. You've got a few exam passes. But they aren't very good, are they?

TOBY: No, sir. I didn't like school very much.

MR. CARTER: Why not? What was wrong with it?

TOBY: It was boring. It didn't have anything to do with real life.

MR. CARTER: Your headmaster and your teachers all say that you could have worked harder.

TOBY: I suppose so. But I didn't get into trouble like some of the others.

MR. CARTER: That's true. Everyone speaks well of you. Now why do you want to come and work for us?

TOBY: I need a job.

MR. CARTER: Any job will do, then?

TOBY: No, sir. I thought this job sounded interesting. I like mechanical things. I've helped my Dad put an old bike together with parts from the scrap yard. It passed its M.o.T. last week.

MR. CARTER: Well done. I see you got a good report from your mechanics teacher. That seems to be the only thing you worked at.

TOBY: And technical drawing.

MR. CARTER: Oh yes. That as well. If you came to work for us, would you be interested in going to night school?

TOBY: What sort of night school? What sort of things would I have to do?

MR. CARTER: Higher National Certificate, basically. We operate a day release scheme for our better trainees. But you'd have to prove yourself at night school before you went on to the day release scheme.

TOBY: That sounds like a good idea. I wouldn't mind night school.

MR. CARTER: Girlfriend wouldn't object?

TOBY: No, sir. She goes to night school herself.

MR. CARTER: Are there any questions you'd like to ask me?

TOBY: Yes, sir. What sort of future does this job have?

MR. CARTER: It's up to you, Toby. If you're prepared to work hard and get some qualifications there's no saying where you might end up. Of course, your pay will go up as you get more experience and qualifications.

TOBY: Has the firm got any clubs or anything like that?

MR. CARTER: We've got a sports ground and a football team.

TOBY: That suits me. I like football.

MR. CARTER: We also have a very good cheap canteen. I eat there myself.

TOBY: That'll make a change from school dinners.

MR. CARTER: No comparison, I should think. Well, if you've got no more questions, Toby . . .

TOBY: I don't think so, sir. You've told me all I want to know.

MR. CARTER: We'll let you know, then.

TOBY: Thank you, sir.

MR. CARTER: Good afternoon.

TOBY: Cheerio, sir.

(*Toby goes out and Miss Pomeroy comes in.*)

MR. CARTER: Has the other young man arrived yet?

MISS POMEROY: Yes, Mr. Carter. He's outside now.

MR. CARTER: Send him in, then.

(*Miss Pomeroy goes out and Clive comes in. Clive sits down without being asked.*)

MR. CARTER: Good afternoon. Clive Rawlins, isn't it? You don't mind if I call you Clive?

CLIVE. Be my guest.

MR. CARTER: I see you've got here at last, Clive. What kept you?

CLIVE: My Dad's car had a puncture.

MR. CARTER: I see. You've had time to clean yourself up, then?

CLIVE: What do you mean?

MR. CARTER: Didn't you help your father change the tyre?

CLIVE: Not me, mate. Never changed a tyre in my life. Don't know how to.

MR. CARTER: Really. Tell me a bit about yourself, Clive.

CLIVE: Not much to tell, really. I've left school. Can't get a job. I just hang about most of the time.

MR. CARTER: Do you read much?

CLIVE: Not much. Comics mostly.

MR. CARTER: Haven't you any hobbies?

CLIVE: Nothing much. I buy a lot of records and listen to them.

MR. CARTER: I see. Now then, I've got your school report here and your application form. Some of your exam marks are quite good. Did you like school?

CLIVE: Not really, but it was something to do. Kept me from getting bored. And anyway my mum wouldn't give me any pocket-money if I didn't get good marks.

MR. CARTER: Yes, your marks are good, but your behaviour seems to leave a lot to be desired.

CLIVE: You can't believe all you read in school reports.

MR. CARTER: I've always found them to be a reliable guide to what youngsters are really like.

CLIVE: The Head really didn't like me. I never got into any real trouble—well apart from that once.

MR. CARTER: Yes, it doesn't seem to be your behaviour they complain about as much as your attitude. Anyway, we'll forget about that for the moment. Tell me, why do you want to come and work for us?

CLIVE: I need the money. Can't live on the dole for ever.

MR. CARTER: Then any job will do?

CLIVE: Well, it depends. I mean, I'm not going to go round emptying dustbins or anything like that.

MR. CARTER: And if you came to work for us, Clive, would you be interested in going to night school?

CLIVE: Day release?

MR. CARTER: No, Clive, night school. We find that if our trainees do a year of night school before they start day release classes, they get more out of their day at the technical college.

CLIVE: It's not what I had in mind. If you're working, you want a bit of fun at night. But if I had to, yes I suppose I'd do it.

MR. CARTER: Have you any questions you'd like to ask me?

CLIVE: It says here the minimum wage. How long do we stay on that?

MR. CARTER: It depends on you. If you work hard and get some qualifications, the rate really goes very high. Let's say by the time you're thirty you should be earning enough to have a nice house and a wife and three kids.

CLIVE: It's not much to start off with though, is it?

MR. CARTER: Because you won't be worth much to the firm when you start, will you? You'll need experience and qualifications if you're going to get on.

CLIVE: I suppose so.

MR. CARTER: One thing I did forget to mention; we have an

excellent sports field. Our football team is in one of the Works Leagues.

CLIVE: No thank you, mate. Had enough of sport at school. I like to watch my sport on the telly.

MR. CARTER: We also have a very good cheap works canteen.

CLIVE: You can keep that and all. I'm fussy about my food.

MR. CARTER: Suit yourself, Clive. Now, is there anything else you'd like to ask while you're here?

CLIVE: I don't think so—it's all in this leaflet, holidays and that.

MR. CARTER: We'll let you know then, Clive. Good afternoon.

CLIVE: Cheerio, then.

(*Clive goes out. Miss Pomeroy comes in.*)

MR. CARTER: Right then, Miss Pomeroy. Two letters—you know the sort of thing—one offering the job and the other—we regret that, etc.

MISS POMEROY: But who gets which, Mr. Carter?

MR. CARTER: Well, Miss Pomeroy, you've also had a chance to talk to these boys. You've worked for me long enough, so surely it's obvious which one I'm going to choose for the job?

JUST THE JOB

Points to Discuss

1. Who do you think got the job? Why did he get it?
2. If you were going for an interview for a job, how would you prepare for it? What would you wear?
3. If you were an employer with three applicants for one job, what qualities would you be looking for as you interviewed them?
4. What do you want out of a job? Do you want to do as little work as possible for as much money as possible? Or do you want a job that you will enjoy, where money is important but not the only consideration?
5. If you could be anything you wanted to be, what job would you choose? Why would you choose that job?

Things to Do

1. Write a letter of application for *one* of the following jobs:

   SCHOOL LEAVER WANTED to train as apprentice in repair shop of large garage. Apply in the first instance to: Mr. E. Blenkinsop, Lovell's Garage, High Street, Maintown. Telephone 59483.

   GIRL WANTED as general clerk in busy office. Good pay and conditions. Apply to: Mrs. Holly, Adman & Rout, High Street, Maintown. Telephone 92841.

2. Make a telephone call to answer one of these advertisements. You could do this in pairs, or your teacher could be the employer.

3. Conduct mock interviews at the Job Centre. What can you do? What are you prepared to do? Again, you could do this in pairs or with your teacher as one of the Job Centre staff.

4. Make a list of all the ways in which you will go about looking for a job—either straight from school, or after leaving your first job.

5. Write down a list of what you could offer an employer— the things you are good at, whether you are dependable, keen, willing, etc. Then list what the employer might offer in return, e.g. staff benefits, security.

SHOPLIFTING

*

Characters

ERROL JOHNS
JIMMY HUGHES
MRS. HARVEY, *Security Officer*
MANAGER OF SUPERSAVER
  DISCOUNT HOUSE
POLICEMAN
MR. HUGHES
MRS. JOHNS
MRS. BENNET, J.P.
MR. PURDIE, J.P.
DR. BROAD, J.P.

Shoplifting

Scene I

Supersaver Discount House

ERROL: Go on, Jimmy, there's nobody looking.

JIMMY: Yes there is. That old woman's watching us.

ERROL: So what? She can't do anything. She's old enough to be my granny's granny.

JIMMY: All the same, I'll wait till she's gone.

ERROL: Suit yourself. If you're chicken, that's your problem.

JIMMY: I'm not chicken. I just think it's stupid to get caught. After all, *you*'ve got what you wanted.

ERROL: O.K., O.K., I know. I'll wait, then.

JIMMY: Never mind. I've got it now.

ERROL: That was quick.

JIMMY: It's the quickness of the hand—and lots of practice, of course. Come on, let's get out of here.

(Mrs. Harvey comes up.)

MRS. HARVEY: Excuse me, boys.

ERROL: It's the little grey-haired old lady.

JIMMY: My granny's granny. What does she want?

ERROL: What do you want, missus?

MRS. HARVEY: I think you've got something there that you haven't paid for.

JIMMY: Oh dear, isn't that naughty? So what are you going to do about it?

MRS. HARVEY: A great deal. I'm the Security Officer at this store. So would you please come with me to the Manager's office.

JIMMY: Not on your life. Come on, Errol.

(*Manager comes in.*)

MANAGER: Not so fast, lads. I've been watching you on the television screen in my office. Well done, Mrs. Harvey. Now, are you going to come along quietly? I wouldn't advise you to try to run away again.

MRS. HARVEY: This way boys, please.

(*All go into the Manager's office.*)

MANAGER: If you would just turn out your pockets, please.

JIMMY: I don't have to if I don't want to. I know my rights.

MANAGER: All right. If that's the way you want to play it, it's all right with me. I'll ring the police now. Whatever you choose to do, you'll have to turn out your pockets sooner or later, either here or at the police station.

ERROL: You'd better do what he says, Jimmy.

JIMMY: All right. Here you are. I suppose this is what you're after?

MANAGER: I think you'd better turn out all your pockets, please. Just to be on the safe side.

JIMMY: But that's all I nicked, honest. Just that one cassette.

ERROL: Just do as he says, Jimmy. There's no need for the aggro bit, is there?

MRS. HARVEY: And now your pockets too, sonny.

ERROL: Who? Me? I ain't nicked nothing, missus. You can't make me turn out my pockets.

MANAGER: Are you going to do as she asks or not?

ERROL: O.K. There you are then. There's not much—a few coppers, a dirty hankie, supporters' club card, fags, matches, odds and ends.

MRS. HARVEY: What about your inside pocket?

ERROL: Nothing in there, missus, honest. Cross my heart.

MRS. HARVEY: Let's see, then.

ERROL: You don't give up, do you? All right, there you are.

MANAGER: That's a nice little radio. It's one of our more expensive lines.

ERROL: It was a present for my Dad.

MANAGER: Oh, I see. Then you'll have a receipt?

ERROL: Lost it.

MANAGER: But I'm sure they'd remember selling it to you. Shall I ring the department and check?

ERROL: Don't bother, mate. I nicked it.

MANAGER: Oh, I say, Mrs. Harvey. Look at that woman in the Food Hall. She's putting more in her bag than she's putting in her trolley.

MRS. HARVEY: I'll go and see to it now, Mr. Phillips.

MANAGER: And now I'd better see about ringing for the police for you two.

Scene II

Magistrates' Court

MR. PURDIE: The next case we have is one of shoplifting brought by the Supersaver Discount House. Are all the parties concerned present? Representative of the shop?

MRS. HARVEY: Yes, sir.

MR. PURDIE: The accused boys?

ERROL/JIMMY: Present, sir.

MR. PURDIE: And the policeman called by the shop?

POLICEMAN: Here, sir.

MR. PURDIE: Good. I think we'll start with the policeman's evidence.

POLICEMAN: I was called to the premises of Supersaver Discount House on Wednesday, 15th September at about 4.30 p.m. The manager had apprehended two · boys for taking objects from his shop and not paying for them.

MRS. BENNET: What were these objects, constable?

POLICEMAN: A music cassette and a transistor radio. I took statements from the boys which you have in front of you now.

MR. PURDIE: Thank you, constable. Can we have the shop representative now, please?

MRS. HARVEY: Yes, sir.

MR. PURDIE: Perhaps you'd like to give us your account of the incident, Mrs. Harvey?

MRS. HARVEY: I thought the boys were behaving in a suspicious manner, so I watched them carefully. It was obvious that they didn't like my watching them, so I turned away. But they didn't realise that I could still see them in a mirror. I saw one of the boys take a cassette out of a basket of cassettes and slip it into his pocket. I then went up to the boys when they tried to leave without paying, and asked them to come to the manager's office.

DR. BROAD: Did they do so willingly?

MRS. HARVEY: No. They tried to run away.

MRS. BENNET: You didn't see the radio being stolen?

MRS. HARVEY: No. We found that on the other boy afterwards.

DR. BROAD: You're sure that the radio came from the shop?

MRS. HARVEY: Certainly. It still had our price tag on it.

MR. PURDIE: Now boys, do you agree with the evidence?

ERROL: The what?

MRS. BENNET: Do you agree with what the policeman and Mrs. Harvey have just said?

ERROL: I suppose so.

DR. BROAD: What about you, Jimmy? Do you agree with what's been said?

JIMMY: Yes, that's about the way it was.

MRS. BENNET: But Jimmy, it doesn't tell us one thing. Why did you do it?

JIMMY: Everybody nicks things.

MRS. BENNET: I certainly don't. I pay for everything I want.

JIMMY: I mean everyone at school, missus.

MR. PURDIE: I'm quite sure that the whole of your school don't spend their spare time shoplifting.

ERROL: He means our mates. They all nick things—fags, sweets and that.

DR. BROAD: And do they get caught?

JIMMY: Sometimes, then that's a risk you've got to take.

MRS. BENNET: So you know the consequences of what you're doing?

ERROL: You don't think about that at the time. You're just thinking about how not to get nicked.

DR. BROAD: So this wasn't the first time you've stolen things from shops.

JIMMY: No, sir. But it was the first time that we've been nicked.

MR. PURDIE: Is there a report from the boys' school?

MRS. BENNET: Yes, there's one here.

DR. BROAD: I see. Poor work, disruptive behaviour. This isn't very good is it, Errol? You know, if you appear before this court again, you will be in very serious trouble. You know that, don't you?

ERROL: Yes, sir.

MRS. BENNET: This other report is quite good. Apart from one thing—truancy. Is this true, Jimmy?

JIMMY: Oh yes, missus. I help my Dad in the yard some days. I'm not really skipping school. I work a lot harder in the yard than I do at school.

MR. PURDIE: I see. Are the parents here?

MRS. JOHNS: Yes, your lordship. I'm here. I'm Errol's mum.

MR. HUGHES: And I'm Jimmy's dad.

MR. PURDIE: Now, Mrs. Johns, what do you think of Errol's behaviour?

MRS. JOHNS: I dunno, I'm sure. I've always brought him up to be a good boy.

MRS. BENNET: Is this the first time that he's been in court?

MRS. JOHNS: Oh yes, your lordship. It's the first time he's been caught.

MR. PURDIE: Does that mean he's stolen things before and not been caught.

MRS. JOHNS: Oh no, your lordship. My boy's a good boy. It's the bad company he keeps what's led him astray.

MR. HUGHES: You keep my lad out of this, missus. Your lad will go astray if he wants, but don't blame my son for it.

MRS. BENNET: And do you have any trouble with him at home?

MRS. JOHNS: Who doesn't have trouble at home with their teenage kids, missus?

DR. BROAD: I think what Mrs. Bennet means is, is your son a disruptive influence in the house?

MRS. JOHNS: I don't know what that is, but I've said before and I'll say it again, he's a good boy he is.

MR. PURDIE: And what about you, have you any problems with your son at home?

MR. HUGHES: My only problem is these teachers who say my Jimmy has to stay at school till he's sixteen. He'd be better off helping me in the yard.

MR. PURDIE: Quite so, Mr. Hughes, but we can't do anything about that here.

MRS. BENNET: What have the boys got to say for themselves?

ERROL: I'm sorry I got nicked.

JIMMY: I'm finished with thieving. Honest. I've learned my lesson. It's not worth it.

MR. PURDIE: As this is your first offence, the Bench have decided to give you a conditional discharge.

ERROL: What's that?

MR. PURDIE: If you are caught again, the Bench will not treat you so leniently.

ERROL: That seems fair enough.

MR. PURDIE: Now if you will all please clear the court. Clerk, call the next case please.

(*Mrs. Harvey, Policeman, Mrs. Johns, Errol, Mr. Hughes and Jimmy leave.*)

MRS. HARVEY: Conditional discharge! A wasted morning. They should be locked up.

POLICEMAN: Don't worry, missus. We'll get them next time. They won't be so soft on them another time.

MRS. JOHNS: Aren't you lucky to get off so lightly?

ERROL: Lightly! We're marked men from now on. We'll be hauled in by the cops for anything.

MR. HUGHES: I hope you meant what you said about keeping out of trouble, Jimmy.

JIMMY: You bet I did. There's no point in nicking things if you're going to get nicked yourself.

SHOPLIFTING

Points to Discuss

1. Do you think that Errol and Jimmy will go shoplifting again?
2. What would you do if you saw someone shoplifting?
3. Do you think that the layout of modern shops encourages shoplifting?
4. Do you think that "honesty is the best policy"? Why have there been laws against stealing from earliest times?
5. Is shoplifting the same as stealing, or is it somehow not so serious? Who pays in the end for goods that are "lifted" from shops? How do shops cover themselves for such losses?
6. If you were caught doing something wrong, do you think that you would be fairly and justly treated? What do you consider "fair" and "just"?

Things to Do

1. Make a list of all the ways in which your local shops try to prevent shoplifting.
2. Look at a local paper and see what punishments have been meted out by the Magistrates' Court. Are they fair? Does the punishment fit the crime?
3. If a man is sent to prison, what sort of problems will his wife and family have to face? Describe what happens to a woman when her husband goes to prison and she has to fend for herself.

4. In the play, many of the people who are present at a
   juvenile court were left out. Can you find out who all
   such people are and what their jobs are?

STRIKE!

★

Characters

CHARLIE FERGUS, *Shop steward*
DOUG GRINDLEY
LOU PATON
SAM JAMES
MARK WHITE
CLARA WHITE, *his wife*
POLICEMAN
Workers at Ormerod's bike factory

Strike!

Scene I

The shop floor at Ormerod's bike factory

CHARLIE: And so, in conclusion comrades, in view of the management's attitude on this matter, I recommend—and my union gives me official backing to say this—we take strike action and withdraw our labour until such time as the management sees fit to reinstate the sacked worker, Charles Bradshaw.

DOUG, LOU, SAM: Hear! Hear!

CHARLIE: Now if I can just have a show of hands. Those in favour of strike action? Those against? None! I hereby declare that the members of the Ormerod branch of the T.G.W.U. have unanimously decided to withdraw their labour, with effect from Monday, until our sacked comrade, Charles Bradshaw is reinstated. Thank you comrades.

DOUG: That'll show old Ormerod we mean business!

LOU: Ormerod's can't carry on riding roughshod over us—sacking old Charlie just for having a smoke.

SAM: I didn't see you putting up your hand, Mark.

MARK: I didn't. I don't agree with this strike.

DOUG: You what? You mean that you agree with the management, then?

MARK: No, I don't. But there is a rule that we mustn't smoke in the machine shop. And that's a safety rule—a rule made for our own safety. If Charlie broke the rule and got the sack, then that's his look-out. I don't see why I should be out of pocket because he's been a fool.

DOUG: That's not the point, Mark. It's a matter of principle. The management could have been content with giving him a telling off. Fergus even offered to dock some of his pay and give it to the Union fund as a sort of fine. But the management wouldn't listen. It was sacking or nothing.

SAM: They said they had to set an example.

LOU: Example to us? I should say so. An example to us— don't get caught or you'll get the sack.

MARK: I still don't think that it's worth while going on strike for. The management here are quite fair—better than they were at my old place.

SAM: Listen to him. There's no such thing as a fair management. They're all out to exploit us.

LOU: You just have to look at them to see that they couldn't care less about us—with their nice clean shirts and their soft white hands—never done a proper day's work in their lives, any of them.

DOUG: Sitting in their centrally heated offices while we freeze on the shop floor. Don't talk to me about fair management.

MARK: All right. But surely I'm entitled to my own opinion —even if I am a Union member.

SAM: You can have any opinion you like, mate, as long as you're out on Monday morning with the rest of us.

LOU: We don't want scabs and blacklegs on this shop floor.

MARK: All right. I'll come out on Monday.

DOUG: Come on then, let's go and have a word with Fergus. We'll have to organise a picket line in case there are some others with principles on Monday morning.

Scene II

Mark's house

CLARA: Oh no, Mark! I can't believe it. You can't go on strike now. We're two months behind already in the payments for the suite, and three months behind on the telly. The kids need new shoes. I can't manage on what you earn. How am I going to manage on strike pay?

MARK: You can claim supplementary benefit. And there'll be some tax to come back. Don't worry, love. We'll find a way.

CLARA: I can't go and claim benefit. All those nasty clerks asking private questions.

MARK: It's no more than you're entitled to. I pay in enough in National Insurance every week. It's time we got something back.

CLARA: Well, *you* can go and claim it. I can't. There's that snooty Hilda Lowe works at the Social Security She'll have it all round the town in no time that we're in a mess. And then what'll my mum say?

MARK: It's none of your mum's business.

CLARA: Oh yes it is. She always said I married beneath myself.

MARK: You didn't have much choice at the time, love— with you four months gone with Kevin.

CLARA: Mark, don't you talk like that. You know how it upsets me.

MARK: Come on, love. Look, if I'm on strike, I'll have time to go down to the office and claim all these things.

CLARA: That's just as bad. Everybody will find out all the same. Have you *got* to go on strike?

MARK: Well, it was a unanimous decision.

CLARA: But have *you* got to go on strike?

MARK: I suppose I have to. I don't even agree with this strike in the first place.

CLARA: So you don't want to go on strike?

MARK: Not really. I don't think that it's important enough to go on strike for.

CLARA: Right. Good. Stand up for your principles then. Don't go on strike.

MARK: I can't do that. They'd send me to Coventry.

CLARA: What for?

MARK: They wouldn't speak to me if I tried to break the strike. It's no use even trying. They wouldn't let me through the picket lines.

CLARA: You might at least give it a try. You wouldn't have to do any work. As long as you turned up there every morning they'd have to pay you, wouldn't they?

MARK: I suppose so. But the blokes—they'd never speak to me again.

CLARA: Well, you'd better choose.

MARK: What do you mean, love?

CLARA: You'd better choose between your mates and me. Because if you don't turn up for work on Monday morning, I'm not going to speak to you again. I'll go back to my mother's. I thought I married a man—not a mouse!

Scene III

Outside the factory. Monday morning.

DOUG: Blimey, it's cold. Got any more tea there, Sam?

SAM: Just a drop. I don't know what we're doing here. Nobody's going to turn up.

LOU: It was a unanimous vote, Doug. We're wasting our time.

SAM: And we could be tucked up nice and warm in bed.

DOUG: I'm not so sure. Look, there's someone coming now.

(*Mark comes in.*)

SAM: Hello there, mate. Didn't know it was your turn on the picket line.

LOU: I thought you were down for tomorrow morning.

MARK: I've not come to join the picket line. I've come to go to work.

DOUG: You scab! Haven't you got the guts to stand up and protect your fellow workers?

MARK: It's not a matter of protecting my fellow workers, mate. It's my wife.

LOU: What has she got to do with it?

MARK: She's threatened to leave me if I go on strike.

DOUG: Let her go, then. She's not much of a wife if she can't stand by you at a time like this.

LOU: She wouldn't leave you. She's only playing games. You know what women are like, mate.

MARK: I know what my wife's like. She's not playing games. I tell you for nothing, she'll be off if I don't go to work. Now let me through.

SAM: Sorry, mate. No way. You know we can't let you through. Now just go on home like a good lad and tell your wife that you can't get into the factory.

MARK: I have a right to work if I want to.

DOUG: Not if we're on the picket line you haven't.

MARK: I didn't agree with this strike in the first place, so I don't see why I shouldn't go in to work if I want to.

LOU: Because we say you can't, mate. This strike was unanimous and it's going to stay that way.

MARK: I thought we lived in a free country. I demand my
rights. I want to go through these gates.

DOUG: Clear off, mate—for your own good.

MARK: Stop pushing me around. Keep your hands to yourself.

(*Policeman comes in.*)

POLICEMAN: Now then, what's going on here?

MARK: I want to go to work and I am not being allowed
free passage through the gates.

POLICEMAN: I'm afraid that you'll have to allow this man
through.

DOUG: Who says?

POLICEMAN: I say. But are you sure that you know what
you're doing, mate?

MARK: Of course I do. It's a matter of principle.

POLICEMAN: I'd forget my principles when it comes to getting through a picket line. I know it's my job to get you
through—but I hope you know what it means.

MARK: Is everyone against the right to work? Even the
police?

POLICEMAN: These are your mates. You've got to work with
them. Don't blame me if they try to get their own
back later.

MARK: All I want is the freedom to choose myself whether I
work or not.

POLICEMAN: All right. Have it your own way, mate. But I
won't be around to protect you when they go back to
work. Move along there now. Let this man through!

DOUG: Scab!

LOU: Blackleg!

SAM: Traitor!

Scene IV

The shop floor at Ormerod's bike works. Two weeks later.

DOUG: Well lads, we won. Charlie's back.

SAM: We showed them, didn't we?

LOU: Hey up, here comes White. Not a word.

(*Mark comes in.*)

MARK: Morning!

(*Silence.*)

MARK: Lend me a spanner, Doug.

DOUG: I see City won again.

LOU: I heard it was a good game.

MARK: Can you lend me a spanner, mate?

SAM: But two men sent off in the second half!

MARK: Can anyone lend me a spanner?

DOUG: This machine's a bit stiff.

LOU: Doesn't do it any good to be left idle for a fortnight.

SAM: I'm a bit stiff myself.

MARK: I'll get my own ruddy spanner.

(*Charlie Fergus comes in.*)

CHARLIE: Good morning comrades. And how is our scab and blackleg this morning?

MARK: Do you all have to behave like a bunch of kids just because I wanted to work?

CHARLIE: I have come to speak to you on behalf of my comrades because they are no longer speaking to you. You knew the consequences of what you were doing.

MARK: It was a matter of principle.

CHARLIE: So I believe. And on a matter of principle I have gone to the management and asked for your dismissal.

We cannot have Union activity in this works messed about by one man and his principles.

MARK: That's unfair! Whoever heard of a man being sacked for working? The management will never agree to it.

CHARLIE: They already have. I threatened to call another strike if you were not dismissed. So to cement good relations with the Union, they have decided to declare you redundant.

MARK: There's no justice in the world! First you strike to support a man who endangers your safety and then you chuck a man out for wanting to work. I'd be better off in Russia. At least they don't have unions there!

STRIKE!

Points to Discuss

1. Could the incidents in the play really happen? Or is it satirical and exaggerated? Criticise the plot and say where you think events might have taken a different turn.
2. Do you think Mark was right to stand up for his principles?
3. Were his workmates justified in sending him to Coventry and were the management right to dismiss him?
4. Mark could almost certainly have brought a case for unfair dismissal. How would he have gone about it? He did nothing wrong in the eyes of the law.
5. Discuss the purpose and benefits of union membership? Are there any drawbacks? Is every worker free to join a union or not, as he pleases?
6. Why do you think that women have less union organisation than men—e.g. shopgirls, office workers, etc.? Are they less union-minded?

Things to Do

1. Write down the names of all the trade unions you have heard of. Which are the largest unions? What is the T.U.C.?
2. Find out how much you will have to pay in Social Security contributions when you get a job. What do you get in return for this? Girls—find out what particular benefits a married woman worker is entitled to.

3. Find out how much the average union dues are. How are they collected? Where does the money go? What does the union give you in return for your money? Perhaps the easiest way to do this, would be to look up the address of your nearest large union—the T.G.W.U. for example, and get the information from them.

4. It is sometimes said that industrial troubles today are inherited from the unjust treatment of workers in the past. Find out about the history of the Trade Union movement. Is it true that 'them' and 'us' attitudes persist today? Do you think that workers and management should do more to work together for the good of the firm? How can this be done? Find out about worker relations in other European countries.

IT TAKES TWO TO MAKE A MARRIAGE

★

Characters

CHRISTINE PRESTON
IRIS WILSON
SAMANTHA WEST } *Christine's friends*
CLAIRE COOK
LES BAKER, *who marries Christine*
KEITH HARRIS } *Les's friends*
ANDREW LODGE

It Takes Two to Make a Marriage

Scene I

Christine's house

CHRISTINE: Well girls, how do you like it?

IRIS: Like what? That's not a new dress!

CHRISTINE: Not my dress. The ring—silly! My engagement ring.

SAMANTHA: Engagement ring! Who on earth are you engaged to?

CHRISTINE: Les, of course. Who else?

CLAIRE: Les, of course, she says. Listen to her. You've been going out with half a dozen boys in the last few months.

CHRISTINE: But Les always was the one, really.

IRIS: I seem to remember it was Keith who was the one last week.

SAMANTHA: And Ossie the week before that.

CHRISTINE: You're just jealous that's all. Just because you haven't got engaged yourselves.

CLAIRE: We could all be engaged if we'd said "yes" to the first bloke who asked us.

CHRISTINE: Are you suggesting that Les is the first bloke to ask me?

IRIS: No, we're not. It's only that—well—are you really sure that it is Les that you want to marry?

CHRISTINE: Of course I want to marry Les. I'm wearing his ring, aren't I?

SAMANTHA: There's more to marriage than wearing a ring, Christine.

CHRISTINE: I know that. Honestly, I thought you'd all be pleased for me. After all, I am the first of the gang to get engaged.

CLAIRE: But it isn't a race you know, Christine. And you are a bit young.

CHRISTINE: You lot are worse than my mother. Everyone gets married young nowadays.

IRIS: Yes, to their first husband.

CHRISTINE: What do you mean by that?

IRIS: It's a well known fact that marriages between people under twenty-one are more liable to break up than marriages between older people.

CHRISTINE: You are an old misery, aren't you? Les and I are right for each other.

SAMANTHA: What are you two going to live on?

CHRISTINE: We've both got a decent wage coming in. We'll manage. I've got a bit saved—but that's all going on the wedding.

CLAIRE: Wouldn't it be better to have a quiet wedding and keep the money for a deposit on a house?

CHRISTINE: A girl only gets married once in her life and my wedding's going to be a big affair. You're all going to be bridesmaids.

IRIS: What does Les think about it?

CHRISTINE: Les says it's my wedding and I can have anything I want.

SAMANTHA: As long as he doesn't have to pay for it.

CLAIRE: When's the big day then, Christine?

CHRISTINE: As soon as possible.

IRIS: You're not pregnant, are you?

CHRISTINE: Oh, my godfathers! What a bunch of cats you

are. Can't a girl get married without you lot thinking the worst? We're getting married as soon as possible because we don't see the point of waiting.

SAMANTHA: You don't think you should get to know each other better? He may have some awful habits that you don't know about.

CLAIRE: He might snore.

IRIS: Or pick his nose.

CHRISTINE: We can just as easily get to know each other after we're married. And anyway I'm fed up with living at home. I'm also fed up with all your catty remarks, and if you say another word—I won't have you as bridesmaids.

IRIS: You can't do that Christine. I need a new evening dress.

Scene II

The pub

KEITH: What's this I hear about you getting married, Les?

ANDREW: Yes, Les. What have you been up to?

LES: I've not been up to anything. I'm marrying Christine Preston next month.

KEITH: What's the hurry, then?

LES: There's no hurry. Christine thinks—I mean Christine and I think that there's no point in waiting to get married.

ANDREW: Got a bit put by, have you?

LES: No, we haven't. But we thought we'd save after we got married.

KEITH: Don't you believe it. Two can't live as cheaply as one.

LES: I know. But we're both fed up with living at home.

ANDREW: Where are you going to live, then?

LES: Christine's looking—I mean *we're* looking for a flat.

KEITH: So she's a good cook, your Christine?

LES: I haven't a clue.

ANDREW: You don't even know if she can cook? What are you getting married for then, mate?

KEITH: You can't live on love, you know.

ANDREW: The quickest way to a man's heart is through his stomach.

LES: Oh shut up the pair of you. I'm sure it'll all work out all right.

ANDREW: But why Christine? I don't know what you see in her. Always struck me as being a bit flighty.

LES: You don't know her like I do. She only gives people that impression because she's shy.

KEITH: She didn't seem a bit shy when she went out with me. Quite the opposite.

ANDREW: What are we all talking about Christine for? Let's get down to the serious business of organising the wedding.

LES: Christine is organising all that. I don't have anything to do at all.

KEITH: Yes you have, mate. You have the most important function of all to organise!

LES: What's that?

ANDREW: Your booze-up, of course. Last night of freedom and all that. Now, let's see. If we all put a fiver in the kitty and start off at the *Flying Horse* . . .

Scene III

The Bakers' flat. A few weeks after the wedding.

LES: Oh, Chris. What have you been doing since you got home? This place is a tip.

CHRIS: I'm tired. I've been working hard all day. I can't be bothered cleaning when I get home at night.

LES: All right. I'll give you a hand. What's for supper?

CHRIS: I forgot to get anything. I'll pop down to the chip shop for something.

LES: That's the third time this week we've had to have chips.

CHRIS: Well I haven't got anything else. Take it or leave it.

LES: All right. I'll take it. You go on down to the chip shop and I'll tidy up a bit here.

CHRIS: Give us some money, then.

LES: Money? But we sorted out the housekeeping on Friday. You can't have spent it all by now?

CHRIS: I bought a new dress on Saturday and some make-up. You do want me to look nice, don't you?

LES: Of course I do, Chris. But we're never going to have a place of our own if you go on spending at this rate. We haven't saved a penny since we got married.

CHRIS: But we've had a lot of expenses.

LES: You've had a lot of expenses, you mean. We didn't need to rent a colour television. A black and white would have done me. Or an automatic washing machine —the launderette's all right.

CHRIS: My mum says you never know who might have used the launderette before you—it's not hygienic.

LES: And what good is that huge fridge-freezer when you never do any shopping?

CHRIS: Oh, you're worse than my mum with your nagging.

Everyone's got a washing-machine and a fridge and a freezer. How can I say I haven't got these things when everyone else has?

LES: Because everyone else has the money to pay for them. We haven't.

CHRIS: Then why did you let me buy them in the first place?

LES: Because I stupidly thought that we might use them. I let you have a colour television because I thought we might stay at home in the evenings and watch it. But do we? No. You want to go out nearly every night. That's costing us a fortune for a start. You've got that great washing-machine and I had to wash my own shirt last night. And an empty fridge-freezer because you're too lazy to shop and you don't know how to cook.

CHRIS: I'm sorry, Les. I haven't been a very good wife, have I? Honestly, I'll try to do better. I'll tidy up every night and I'll do the washing and ironing at the weekend.

LES: And from now on we stay in every night, and I'll help you with the cooking.

CHRIS: Every night?

LES: Except Saturdays. I'll even give up my Friday nights with the boys. And old Travers says I can have as much overtime as I like. So it won't take long to save that deposit.

Scene IV

The flat. A few weeks later.

LES: Chris! I'm back. Sorry I'm late, but I got some more overtime. Chris! Where are you? No sign of her. Maybe she's still at the shops. There's the doorbell. Maybe she's forgotten her key.

(*Samantha, Iris, Claire, and Andrew come in.*)

LES: Hello there. Come on in. I've just got back and Chris isn't home.

ANDREW: We know Chris isn't home. That's why we're here.

LES: What's up? She hasn't had an accident or something?

IRIS: No, Les, she hasn't had an accident.

LES: Then where is she?

SAMANTHA: Oh come on. Somebody will have to tell him. She's left you, Les.

LES: Chris left me? Impossible. She was here last night.

CLAIRE: But she's not here now. She's gone off with Keith.

LES: With Keith? What on earth for?

IRIS: She got fed up with not going out.

SAMANTHA: All that overtime you've been doing—it left her on her own a lot.

CLAIRE: We tried to keep her company, Les, but she didn't really want us.

LES: But why didn't she tell me?

IRIS: Come off it, Les. She says she never stopped moaning at you about the hours you worked.

LES: She never mentioned it once. I thought she was happy. I was only doing it for her. We've got nearly £500 saved now. That's funny. The building society book was here this morning.

ANDREW: Whose name is it in?

LES: It's joint. Where the heck is it?

ANDREW: I think you'll find that's gone too.

LES: The bitch! The sneaky little bitch!

IRIS: Don't worry, Les. I think you can get your money back if you get in touch with the building society in the morning.

LES: I don't want my money back. All I want is my wife.

ANDREW: I very much doubt that, Les.

IRIS: This affair with Keith has been going on for quite a while now.

CLAIRE: Ever since you started working overtime.

SAMANTHA: I don't think Chris meant it to go as far as this at the beginning.

ANDREW: I think she was just lonely and Keith cheered her up.

LES: But if you all knew about it, why didn't you tell me?

IRIS: You know how it is, Les. We didn't want to interfere.

ANDREW: Would you go up to a bloke and say, 'Hey, your wife's having an affair with your best friend'?

LES: But if I'd known, I could have done something about it.

ANDREW: Could you? I doubt it. If it hadn't been Keith, it would have been somebody else. Chris wasn't in love with you—she was in love with the idea of being in love.

IRIS: And once the daily realities of marriage hit her, she couldn't take it.

SAMANTHA: She wanted a wedding—she didn't want a marriage.

CLAIRE: You've been too good for her, Les.

LES: So you think she's gone for good? What'll I do with all this stuff?

ANDREW: I was hoping you'd get round to that. I'll make you a fair offer for the lot.

LES: What do you want with a fridge-freezer and a washing-machine?

IRIS: A great deal! Andrew and I are getting married next month.

LES: As an old married man, let me give you some advice, mate . . .

ANDREW: What's that? Don't do it?

LES: No. Don't work overtime!

IT TAKES TWO TO MAKE
A MARRIAGE

Points to Discuss

1. Were Les and Christine right to spend so much money on the wedding?
2. The girl in the play thought that "getting married" was the thing to do. Do you think that such a big fuss should be made of the ceremony?
3. Do you think that marriage is a thing of the past?
4. Marriage isn't easy and everyone goes through "bad patches". Should divorce be made more simple or more difficult to get?
5. Should a married woman receive payment for housework? Who would pay it?
6. Do you think that computer dating can really select a suitable marriage partner?

Things to Do

1. If a marriage has problems, advice can be obtained from the Marriage Guidance Council. Find out all you can about this organisation.
2. Do you know what you have to do before you can get married? Do you need your parents' consent? What officials do you have to see? What things have to be organised for a church wedding? How much does it all cost?
3. What happens when people get divorced? What financial settlements are made? What happens to children in a

divorce? Try to find out the answers to these questions. You will find that there is no such thing as an easy divorce.

4. Draw up a list of famous people—many of them in the entertainment world—who have been married many times. Say whether you think these marriages can be compared with those of ordinary people. Have they the same meaning or commitment? Explain your reasons.

FLAT SHARING

*

Characters

MRS. KELLY, *the landlady*
AMANDA HUDSON
BETTY PRICE
PHIL SYME, *Betty's boyfriend*
EDDIE GARDINER

Flat Sharing

Scene I

The bedsitter

MRS. KELLY: Well, here it is, girls. Take it or leave it. If you don't want it there are dozens that do. Double bedsitter, with your own kitchen. Share the bathroom with the rest of the landing.

AMANDA: Thanks, Mrs. Kelly. It's very nice.

BETTY: Yes, very nice indeed.

MRS. KELLY: Well, do you want it or do you not? Now if you do want it, we'll have no young men after eleven o'clock at night. This is a respectable house, this is.

AMANDA: Do you think we could discuss it for a minute, Mrs. Kelly?

MRS. KELLY: Please yourselves. Knock on my door on the way out. It's the last on your right before the front door.

BETTY: Thank you Mrs. Kelly. We won't be a minute.

(*Mrs. Kelly goes out.*)

BETTY: What do you think? It's a bit grotty, isn't it?

AMANDA: It's not half as bad as some of the places we've looked at. And it's cheap.

BETTY: You can see why it's cheap. Look at this bed. It's got more lumps than school custard.

AMANDA: And this sofa! Blimey! Look at the dust.

BETTY: This is a respectable house, this is. No young men after eleven o'clock.

AMANDA: What about old men?

BETTY: Are we having it or are we not?

AMANDA: I can't stand staying at home for much longer. My mum's driving me crazy with her nag, nag, nag.

BETTY: And I hate that hostel. Look, we can give this a try while we look for something better. At least we can have a bit of freedom here.

AMANDA: Freedom! No more "Be home by ten o'clock" and "Who's the boyfriend today?"

BETTY: Home cooking! Boyfriends to visit!

AMANDA: Until eleven o'clock—remember. This is a respectable house. I can't wait to tell Ian.

BETTY: Once we've moved in, we'll have to sit down and work out a proper budget.

AMANDA: And we'll have to keep to it. This place may be cheap—but we've still got to fork out a lot of our pay in rent.

BETTY: Come on, let's go and tell Mrs. Kelly the glad news. She's rented her grotty bedsit—to a respectable couple!

Scene II

The bedsitter. Three weeks later.

PHIL: What are we waiting for, Betty? I'm starving.

BETTY: Amanda's gone to meet Ian. He hasn't been here before and he doesn't know the way.

PHIL: How's the flat going? Are you two hitting it off all right?

BETTY: Yes, I suppose so. Amanda's no housewife. She can't cook and she's awfully untidy. But it's all right.

PHIL: She can't cook? Does that mean you've got to do all the cooking?

BETTY: At the moment I do. But she's learning. This morning she actually managed to boil an egg.

PHIL: That sounds like them now.

(*Amanda and Eddie come in.*)

BETTY: What's happened to Ian?

AMANDA: Oh, I couldn't wait all day for him to turn up. This is Eddie. Phil and Betty.

EDDIE: Hello there. Nice to meet you both.

BETTY: Hello, Eddie. But why haven't you brought Ian?

AMANDA: Oh, Betty, you're worse than my mother. Eddie came along while I was waiting for Ian. We got talking, and here he is.

PHIL: Let's cut the explanations and eat. I'm hungry.

BETTY: Five minutes, Phil. I've just got a few things to do.

EDDIE: You go ahead, Betty. It sure smells delicious.

PHIL: Are you an American?

EDDIE: Gosh, no. But I work in the pop music business. I arrange tours for the big stars.

AMANDA: Eddie's somebody, you see.

BETTY: Do you meet the pop stars?

EDDIE: Of course I do, every day. They're a great bunch of guys.

PHIL: I thought they were all poufs or junkies.

EDDIE: Not at all. They're all regular guys.

PHIL: They eat the right breakfast cereal, then?

AMANDA: You should see Eddie's car. Big and American. It's lovely.

PHIL: I bet it uses a lot of petrol though. And parking must be a problem.

EDDIE: I can afford it. When you're with the stars—even traffic wardens turn a blind eye.

BETTY: It sounds a fantastic job, Eddie.

EDDIE: I don't know. It gets a bit boring after a while—New

York one week, Vegas the next. That's when you really begin to appreciate the atmosphere of a pad like this.

PHIL: You dig boiled cabbage and dust, do you?

EDDIE: But it's homely, man. Those hotels—they're all the same. Surly room service, iced water and you know the menu without bothering to read it. Give me home cooking every time.

PHIL: I don't know how you can tear yourself away from the bright lights.

EDDIE: Well—to tell the truth ... I'm keeping a bit of a low profile at the moment. I had a bit of a disaster at the sauna today.

AMANDA: Tell them. Eddie was robbed!

PHIL: I weep for him.

BETTY: Oh Phil, don't be so rude.

EDDIE: Yeah, they took me for all I had. Wallet, credit cards, the lot. I had just drawn out my last penny for a new pad in Kensington. I've already moved in my gear and cleared out of my old pad. Now the agent won't give me the key. No money—no key!

AMANDA: So Eddie's got no money and nowhere to go!

BETTY: Well he can't stay here. This is a respectable house, this is.

PHIL: Stop looking at me, Amanda. He can't stay at my place either.

EDDIE: It's only tonight, till I can raise some ante tomorrow. Heck, I can go to Rod and get a grand any time I like.

AMANDA: Not *the* Rod ...?

EDDIE: Who else? He's a great buddie of mine.

AMANDA: Why don't we lend you some money, Eddie, just so you can find a place for the night?

EDDIE: I couldn't take money from you. I hardly even know you.

BETTY: That's the best idea, Amanda. We've got the rent money all ready. You can borrow that until tomorrow, Eddie.

EDDIE: Gee, that's awful kind of you girls. I can shack up in a cheap pad for the night and pay you back tomorrow.

PHIL: You'll be lucky.

(*Knock at the door.*)

BETTY: I'll go. (*Mrs. Kelly comes in.*) Hello Mrs. Kelly.

MRS. KELLY: I hope I'm not interrupting anything. Having a party are you? That smells nice. Don't forget, these boys have to be out by eleven. This is a respectable house, this is.

BETTY: Yes, Mrs. Kelly. Of course, Mrs. Kelly. Now what can we do for you?

MRS. KELLY: It's about the rent. I've got to go and visit my married sister tomorrow—she's been taken poorly. So can I have the rent tonight instead of tomorrow—if it's all the same to you?

AMANDA: Oh dear, Mrs. Kelly, I'm afraid you can't.

BETTY: We've just lent it to Eddie here. He's been robbed and has nowhere to go.

MRS. KELLY: Eddie, is it? Don't I know you? Yes I do! You're one of Edna Bolton's: second floor back. Ran off owing six weeks' rent. But Eddie wasn't your name then. Frank it was . . . Frank Hale.

EDDIE: The old bird's flipped her lid.

AMANDA: There must be some mistake, Mrs. Kelly. Eddie's a pop star agent.

MRS. KELLY: He's unemployed. He was a bookie's clerk and he got the sack for fiddling the books. Edna pointed you out to me many a time. You didn't see me behind those lace curtains of hers. But I saw you. Frank Hale. Fancy that.

EDDIE: Well thanks for the bread, girls. I've got to blow.

AMANDA: What about our money?

EDDIE: You'll get that back. Don't worry.

PHIL: They're not going to worry. You're going to give it straight back.

AMANDA: Oh Phil, you're hurting him!

PHIL: I don't care. The lying cheat. Frank Hale, is it? Hand over that money—or Mrs. Kelly will phone the police.

MRS. KELLY: I'm not sure about the police. This is a respectable house.

EDDIE: Let go of my arm. You're hurting me.

PHIL: Not till you hand over that money.

EDDIE: All right. Here you are.

(*Eddie goes out.*)

PHIL: Here you are, Mrs. Kelly. Rent money, all present and correct.

MRS. KELLY: It's a good job I came in when I did. You'd never have seen that money again. Pop stars indeed!

PHIL: And you two were nearly conned out of your rent money. You know you're too innocent to be left on your own.

MRS. KELLY: There's the phone ringing now. I'd better go and answer it.

AMANDA: It might be Ian. I'll come with you Mrs. Kelly.

(*Mrs. Kelly and Amanda go out.*)

BETTY: I think she owes Ian an apology.

PHIL: And you owe me an apology. I could see right through that Eddie.

BETTY: I know you could. But don't ram it down our throats. Thank goodness Mrs. Kelly recognised him.

(*Amanda comes in.*)

AMANDA: Great news! Ian's found a flat for us. A proper flat. No landlady. Living room. Own bathroom. Two bedrooms.

BETTY: We can't afford that.

AMANDA: We can, if we get two other girls to share.

BETTY: They'll have to be able to cook. I'm not cooking for four.

PHIL: You won't have to. And you're not going to find another two girls either. Ian and I talked about this last night. We didn't think you two were capable of looking after yourselves. After this business with Eddie—we know you're not capable of looking after yourselves.

BETTY: So what are you going to do about it?

PHIL: We are going to share the flat with you.

AMANDA: Mrs. Kelly wouldn't like that it's not respectable.

PHIL: It's going to be more respectable than being fleeced by every con-man in the business.

FLAT SHARING

Points to Discuss

1. Would you have been taken in by Eddie? Do you believe everything that is said to you? How would you check that someone is genuine—for example, if like Eddie, he said he worked in the pop world?
2. What do you think the main problems would be if you shared a flat with friends?
3. Do you think that mixed flat sharing is a good idea? Why? Or why not?
4. At what age should you leave home and start to live in a flat?
5. If you were a landlord or landlady letting out a flat to young people what would be fair and reasonable conditions to make?
6. What would you do about noisy neighbours with lots of parties? And what would you do if the neighbours complained about you?

Things to Do

1. Write down how you would go about looking for a flat.
2. Make a list of questions you should ask the landlord.
3. Find out what are the duties of a Rent Tribunal.
4. What would be your priorities in working out a budget if you had a flat. If you earned £50 a week, how would you allocate your money?
5. Are there differences in renting furnished and unfurnished accommodation? Find out some of the main

points of the Rent Act and how they affect landlord and tenant.

6. When Eddie left his 'pad' owing six weeks' rent could Mrs. Bolton have got her money back? Find out about the legal position.

IT'S ALL IN THE GAME

★

Characters

CARL DAVIES
PATRICK MARSH, *his friend*
MR. DAVIES
MRS. DAVIES
GRAHAM SHARPE ⎫
MICK STAFFORD ⎬ *Football rowdies*
PHIL JOHNSON ⎭
SERGEANT SANDERS
P.C. ROBINSON

It's All in the Game

Scene I

The Davies' house

PATRICK: Are you ready then, Carl?

CARL: In a minute. I've just got to get my scarf.

MRS. DAVIES: I do wish you'd stop going to football matches, Carl. You'll get into trouble one of these days—like that Graham Sharpe and his gang.

CARL: Oh Mum, don't be daft. Don't believe all you read in the newspapers. And anyway Graham Sharpe supports United. They're a right bunch of hooligans.

MR. DAVIES: Your mother's right, Carl. Respectable folk can't go to watch a match any more. I don't like you going either.

PATRICK: Don't worry, Mr. Davies. Carl and I can look after ourselves.

MRS. DAVIES: That's just what I'm afraid of. You'll get into trouble with the police. I'm not saying you'd start trouble, but who knows what you might get up to if someone provoked you?

CARL: I should think we'd run. Now don't worry, Mum. We'll keep well away from the rowdies.

MR. DAVIES: I don't know why you go on supporting a team like City anyway. They haven't spent a penny on that ground since I was a lad. They'll spend a hundred thousand on a player, but they won't put out a farthing to build some decent bogs.

PATRICK: You're right, there, Mr. Davies. The ground *is* a bit of a dump.

MRS. DAVIES: There's no point in spending good money on the ground when these hooligans would just wreck it.

CARL: Right, Patrick, I'm ready. O.K., we're off. And don't worry, Mum.

MRS. DAVIES: I can't help it. Now, hurry back and don't hang about the streets after the match.

Scene II

The City football ground

PATRICK: Good crowd here today.

CARL: Makes a change. The gates have been pathetic this year.

PATRICK: Look at that lot behind the City goal. They're packed solid.

CARL: The cops are moving some of them out.

PATRICK: Oh no! Here comes Sharpe and his gang.

CARL: What are they doing here? United are playing away aren't they?

PATRICK: Probably can't afford to go anywhere this weekend after the fines they had to pay last week.

(*Sharpe, Stafford and Johnson come in.*)

SHARPE: Look who's here. It's namby pamby Davies.

CARL: Clear off, Sharpe. We want to watch the game.

STAFFORD: We've got as much right here as you have. We've paid for our tickets—same as you.

PATRICK: What are United supporters doing at a City match anyway?

JOHNSON: Thought we'd come and watch the opposition for a change.

CARL: They've probably banned you from United's matches after last weekend's punch-up.

SHARPE: And what do you mean by that?

CARL: You didn't exactly behave like a Sunday School outing, now did you?

SHARPE: Watch it, mate.

JOHNSON: Cool it Graham. So what? We got done. Why not? That's what it's all about, isn't it?

PATRICK: It may be for you. But we came to watch the football. Clear off and join the other rowdies.

SHARPE: Listen to him! Join the other rowdies, he says. Not good enough for you, are we? We'll see about that. Grab their scarves.

PATRICK: Get off and leave me alone!

CARL: Don't touch me—or you'll regret it.

SHARPE: Listen to him—couldn't beat a ruddy egg, he couldn't.

PATRICK: Let's see you fight then. Come on—try it!

CARL: Ignore them, Patrick. Push off, Sharpe, and take your bully boys with you.

SHARPE: Scared are you? Scared we'll beat the living daylights out of you?

PATRICK: You heard what he said. Clear off!

JOHNSON: Well if you won't fight, let's see what you'll do about this.

PATRICK: He's got a knife.

JOHNSON: Now, are you going to hand over that scarf?

SHARPE: That's the way Phil. Now we've got them!

CARL: Put that knife away before somebody gets hurt.

JOHNSON: Don't you think that I won't use it—I will if I'm provoked. Now are you going to hand over that scarf?

PATRICK: Watch out, Carl. He's coming at you! Duck!

CARL: You stupid idiot! Stop mucking about with that knife.

STAFFORD: Argh!

SHARPE: What's happened?

JOHNSON: I don't know. Davies moved, and I sort of lost my balance, fell on Mick, and somehow I've knifed him. It was an accident. You all saw that, didn't you? I didn't mean to hurt anyone. I was only kidding. Honest.

CARL: Come on Patrick. Let's get out of here. Accident or no accident, I don't want to get mixed up in this.

SHARPE: Come back, you two. If you let on about what happened, I'll personally carve up the pair of you.

PATRICK: Don't worry mate, we won't say a word.

Scene III

The Davies' house

MR. DAVIES: It says in the paper here that a lad was stabbed at the match today.

MRS. DAVIES: Oh, no! I always said that those rowdies don't know where to stop.

MR. DAVIES: Did you see any of it, Carl?

CARL: Oh no, Dad. It was very quiet down our end, wasn't it, Patrick?

PATRICK: Yes it was Mr. Davies. Very quiet.

MR. DAVIES: Good game, then?

CARL: So so. It had its moments.

MRS. DAVIES: Well that's everything tidied up. I'm off out to the bingo. Don't you two get up to any mischief while I'm out.

CARL: We won't, Mum. We're not going anywhere.

MRS. DAVIES: Are you going down to the pub, Fred?

MR. DAVIES: I might wander down later. Yes dear.

MRS. DAVIES: See you there, then. Cheerio.

    (*Goes out.*)

MR. DAVIES: I suppose I'd better have a wash before I go out. Can't go down the pub with a five o'clock shadow.

    (*Goes out.*)

CARL: Where's Dad's paper?

PATRICK: Here it is. Look. Teenage boy stabbed at match. Condition is said to be serious.

CARL: Poor old Mick!

PATRICK: What do you mean? Poor old Mick! It might have been us.

CARL: Not Mick. He's not really one of that gang, he's just a bit simple and easily led.

PATRICK: But what are we going to do?

CARL: Well you heard what Sharpe said. He'll carve us up if we tell anyone. He's not a bloke that's known for empty promises. Look what he did to Bruce Lake last year.

PATRICK: And that was just for going out with Sharpe's girlfriend.

CARL: We'll have to keep our mouths shut. I don't think we'll have any problem. Sharpe's got such a reputation with the police they'll never believe a word he says.

PATRICK: I hope you're right. (*Knock at the door.*) Somebody at the door.

CARL: It'll be one of Dad's boozing cronies I expect. I'll go.

    (*Goes out.*)

MR. DAVIES: (*Off.*) Who's at the door, son?

PATRICK: Carl's gone to see.

CARL: (*Comes in with Sgt. Sanders and P.C. Robinson.*) It's the police!

SGT. SANDERS: Is your dad at home, son?

CARL: He's upstairs. Do you want him?

SGT. SANDERS: No, son, it's you we've come to see. But we like the parents to be there when we're talking to kids.

CARL: Kids? What have we done?

SGT. SANDERS: Just call your old man down, will you, son?

CARL: Dad, that was the police at the door. They want you down here.

P.C. ROBINSON: Who's this?

CARL: My mate. Patrick Marsh.

SGT. SANDERS: Was he at the match too?

PATRICK: Yes I was. I was with Carl.

SGT. SANDERS: Then we'd better call on your dad as well when we're through here.

CARL: Wait a minute, sergeant. We haven't done anything wrong. What's all this about?

SGT. SANDERS: A young lad was stabbed at the match this afternoon.

CARL: Yes, we know. We were just reading about it in the papers. Here's my dad now.

(*Mr. Davies comes in.*)

DAD: What's going on here?

SGT. SANDERS: Evening, Mr. Davies. I'm Sergeant Sanders, and this is P.C. Robinson. We've come to have a word with your young lad here.

MR. DAVIES: What's he been up to?

SGT. SANDERS: He says he hasn't been up to anything. But

we've got someone who says that he might know something about the stabbing this afternoon.

P.C. ROBINSON: In fact our friend says that young Carl here was the one who put the knife into Stafford.

PATRICK: Your friend wouldn't be Graham Sharpe would he?

SGT. SANDERS: So you do know something about it?

CARL: Well . . .

SGT. SANDERS: Come on lad. Out with it!

PATRICK: Can we get police protection?

P.C. ROBINSON: Protection? Who from? The Mafia aren't in this as well?

CARL: It's not funny, I can tell you.

SGT. SANDERS: Let's have your story then and we'll see whether you need protecting or not.

CARL: All right. We met Sharpe and his gang at the match this afternoon.

PATRICK: We told them to push off, but they wouldn't leave us alone.

CARL: They started pinching our scarves. They're not City supporters like us, you see.

PATRICK: They wanted a fight. We tried to put them off.

CARL: Then Phil pulled a knife.

SGT. SANDERS: Phil Johnson?

PATRICK: That's right. He aimed it at Carl. But Carl ducked and it hit Mick instead.

CARL: And we ran.

PATRICK: Sharpe threatened to "carve us up" if we split on him.

P.C. ROBINSON: So that's where the protection comes in, is it?

CARL: He roughed up Bruce Lake last year, and he wasn't a pretty sight by the time old Sharpe and his gang had finished with him.

SGT. SANDERS: Would you like to come down to the station and make a statement?

PATRICK: Does that mean that we'll have to give evidence?

P.C. ROBINSON: Yes, lad, it does. Are you scared?

CARL: We're not scared of giving evidence. But we are scared of what Sharpe will do to us. He wasn't the one with the knife.

PATRICK: So he'll get off lightly.

SGT. SANDERS: No, he won't. Aiding and abetting an assault with a deadly weapon—with his record, I think we'll get him put away for a few years.

CARL: How's Mick?

SGT. SANDERS: He'll live. Luckily it didn't hit anything vital. I think this will be the end of Sharpe's gang, though.

PATRICK: Thank goodness for that.

P.C. ROBINSON: Why didn't you lads come and tell us about it earlier?

CARL: We were scared. But you didn't really believe Sharpe when he said that we had done it?

SGT. SANDERS: Of course not. Johnson's prints were on the knife. But we needed evidence. Witnesses. Statements.

P.C. ROBINSON: And now, thanks to you, we've got them.

SGT. SANDERS: But next time you see anything, lads, don't wait for us to find you. It makes our job a lot easier if you come clean right away.

IT'S ALL IN THE GAME

Points to Discuss

1. Do you think that Carl and Patrick should have gone to the police right away?
2. Why does football attract rowdy spectators? Are they really interested in the game?
3. Are Britain's football grounds in need of modernisation?
4. What's wrong with the game of football today?
5. Do you think that violence on the pitch encourages violence on the terraces?
6. Do you believe that football hooliganism is a local, a national or an international problem? What are the causes and how can it be tackled? Can you suggest new ways that have not yet been tried?

Things to Do

1. Find out what your local football club is doing to prevent football rowdyism.
2. Find out how much your local club spent on facilities last year. Find out how much it spent on players. Do you think that it has its priorities right?
3. Make a list of improvements that you think your local club needs. (You can't do anything about the players!)
4. Find out the gate at the last football match at your local club. If it was low, why was it low?
5. Do a survey of some of the people in your town. Why do they go to football matches? Did they ever go to football matches? Why did they stop going to football matches?
6. Invite a senior member of your local police force to talk about the problems of football spectators and other instances of violence, like vandalism.

THE CAR

★

Characters

MARTIN BROWN
JENNY TAYLOR
MR. BROWN
MRS. BROWN
SETH GRAHAM
POLICEMAN

The Car

Scene I

The Browns' house

MARTIN: I've passed!

MRS. BROWN: Congratulations, dear. What have you passed?

MARTIN: My driving test, Mum. I passed first time.

MR. BROWN: So what. Any fool can pass a driving test. I don't know what things are coming to, when they let young fools like you loose on the roads. I'm not letting you borrow my car.

MARTIN: And I'm not asking you for it. I'm buying my own. I've been saving up for a year now.

MRS. BROWN: Do you think you should, dear? You'd be better off putting that money in the bank—or in a building society.

MARTIN: For goodness sake, Mum! You're only young once. Why can't I have a car? It's my money and I've worked hard for it.

MRS. BROWN: I was thinking of Jenny.

MARTIN: Jenny is a hundred per cent behind me about buying a car. She's tired of standing in the rain waiting for buses that never come.

MR. BROWN: You just want to use that car for your courting, that's all. You don't really need a car.

MARTIN: I need a car to get about, Dad. Now can I have a look at the paper to see what's for sale?

MR. BROWN: Why don't you buy a car from a respectable garage—not one of those fly-by-night advertisers?

MARTIN: Don't worry Dad, I know what I'm doing.

MR. BROWN: It's your money, lad. You can do what you like with it. I wash my hands of the whole affair.

Scene II

A street

JENNY: Are you sure it's such a bargain?

MARTIN: Well, you have a look. Mini, four years old, low mileage—and look at the price.

JENNY: That's £200 less than they want at Brooke's garage for that red Mini.

MARTIN: And that's four years old as well. Can't be bad, can it?

JENNY: But Brooke's garage can give you some sort of guarantee. What can this chap give you?

MARTIN: It doesn't matter, Jenny. You can't go wrong. It's all covered by the Trade Descriptions Act. All you need is the M.o.T.

JENNY: Are you sure?

MARTIN: Of course I'm sure. That's what the M.o.T.'s for, isn't it?

JENNY: Forty-seven, forty-nine. Looks like we're here. Forty-nine Acacia Drive. That's the address in the advertisement, isn't it?

MARTIN: And that must be the car. Looks nice, doesn't it?

JENNY: Nice and shiny. But you'd make a car nice and shiny if you were going to sell it, wouldn't you?

MARTIN: Let's have a look at it before we ring the bell.

(*Seth Graham comes out.*)

SETH: You the bloke that rang about the car?

MARTIN: That's right. Martin Brown. I'm just having a look at it.

SETH: Help yourself. Breaks my heart to sell her. I'm emigrating you see. Off to Australia. That car's been my pride and joy for the last year. But I need the money to pay my fare.

MARTIN: Can I have a ride in her?

SETH: Of course. Lovely runner she is. Does your lady friend want to come as well?

JENNY: Yes please.

SETH: Hop in the back then.

(*All three get in the car.*)

SETH: Are you insured, mate?

MARTIN: No, not yet. I haven't got a car.

SETH: Well I'd better drive then. Now you can see what nice condition she's in. Fitted carpets, those mats as well, and the extras—radio, cigar lighter.

MARTIN: I don't smoke.

SETH: Never mind. Heated rear window—the lot. This is a real luxury car. Listen to that engine. Purrs like a cat!

JENNY: It is quiet, isn't it?

MARTIN: What about the brakes?

SETH: No problem at all. Look at that. Instant stop. Complete control.

MARTIN: You have got an M.o.T. for her?

SETH: Almost a full year to go, mate. It's in the glove compartment there. O.K. then, here we are back at the house.

MARTIN: Mind if I have a look underneath?

SETH: Help yourself mate. All in tip-top condition there too.

(*They all get out of the car.*)

SETH: I'll just go into the house for the log book.

   (*Seth goes out.*)

JENNY: What are you looking at?

MARTIN: I'm trying to see what it's like underneath. Looks O.K. Tyres look quite new too. What do you think of it, Jenny?

JENNY: I don't know. I don't like the bloke. His eyes are too close together.

MARTIN: Oh, Jenny. Just like a woman! I'm buying a car. What have that bloke's eyes got to do with it?

JENNY: I'm just saying what I think. Go ahead and do what you like. But don't say I didn't warn you.

   (*Seth comes back.*)

SETH: Here you are mate, log book. Only two owners from new.

MARTIN: You bought the car secondhand, did you?

SETH: That's right. Done a lot of work to her, too. What do you think then, mate? Are you interested?

MARTIN: It seems such a bargain. Yes, I'll have her.

SETH: Fine. Come on in the house and we'll discuss the details.

Scene III

In the car. A week later.

MRS. BROWN: It's a nice car, Martin. You've got to admit that, haven't you, Archie?

MR. BROWN: It's all right, I suppose.

MRS. BROWN: And I think Martin was so clever, getting it so cheap and all.

JENNY: He managed to knock off another £50 when he was paying for it.

MARTIN: Jenny didn't want me to buy it. She said the bloke's eyes were too close together.

MRS. BROWN: Look, Martin. What's that up ahead?

MR. BROWN: It looks like an accident. What a lot of police.

MARTIN: No it isn't. It's one of those spot checks.

MRS. BROWN: He's waving at us!

MARTIN: Wants us to pull in.

MRS. BROWN: Oh dear, what if he finds anything wrong with the car?

MARTIN: Don't worry, Mum. The car's in perfect condition.

POLICEMAN: Good afternoon, sir. We're conducting spot checks on the roadworthiness of cars. I hope you won't mind if we check yours.?

MARTIN: Not at all. Go ahead. I've only just bought the car.

POLICE: Do you have the registration book and the M.o.T.?

MARTIN: Yes, here they are.

POLICEMAN: It would be easier for our boys if you all got out of the car, sir. If you don't mind.

MARTIN: Of course not. We need a bit of fresh air. Come on. Everybody out.

(*Martin, Jenny and the Browns get out of the car.*)

POLICEMAN: This won't take a minute, sir.

(*Goes out.*)

MRS. BROWN: What a way to spend a Saturday afternoon. Standing on the motorway watching policemen check cars.

MR. BROWN: It's all part of their job. Somebody has to do it. Can't have the roads littered with old heaps.

JENNY: Martin. That policeman doesn't look too happy about your car.

MARTIN: Nonsense. Policemen never look happy anyway.

MR. BROWN: The lass is right. Look, he's called another one over.

MRS. BROWN: Oh, Martin. What's wrong?

MARTIN: Stop fussing, Mum. That car's in perfect running order.

(*Policeman comes in.*)

POLICEMAN: Excuse me, sir, would you mind stepping over here?

MARTIN: Not at all.

POLICEMAN: We'd like to show you something. Just bought the car you say?

MARTIN: Yes, last week.

POLICEMAN: From a dealer?

MARTIN: No it was a private sale. An ad. in the newspaper.

POLICEMAN: You didn't have it checked by the A.A., then?

MARTIN: No I didn't. It's got an M.o.T. That's enough.

POLICEMAN: That's what they all say. Don't you ever read the small print? The M.o.T. is no guarantee that a car is roadworthy.

MARTIN: But mine's all right. Isn't it?

POLICEMAN: I'm afraid not, sir. Take a look at this. It's been patched up after a crash I would say. The whole chassis is bent. Take a look at the tyres.

MARTIN: But those tyres were almost new!

POLICEMAN: But look at the wear on them already. Bent chassis always does that.

MARTIN: Is that all?

POLICEMAN: All? You can't drive a car with a bent chassis like that.

MARTIN: But I can get it repaired, can't I?

POLICEMAN: Not worth it, son. It would cost more than the car's worth. If I were you I'd sell this car for scrap. Subframe's rusted through and I wouldn't trust those brakes, not even at five miles an hour.

MARTIN: Well I can drive my parents home in it, can't I?

POLICEMAN: Sorry, sir. We can't even let you do that. We'll tow it to the police garage for you and give you a lift home in one of our cars. You'd be risking your life driving that car—and other people's lives as well.

MARTIN: What am I going to tell my parents?

POLICEMAN: You've been done, son!

THE CAR

Points to Discuss

1. What should Martin do now? Is there any way he can get his money back?
2. An M.o.T. Test Certificate is not a guide to the condition of a car. In what other ways can you check that a car you want to buy is in good condition?
3. Which is better when buying a car—hire purchase or cash? What are the advantages and disadvantages of each method?
4. What sort of car would you like to buy and why?
5. What is wrong with the motor-car as a means of transport? What would be better?

Things to Do

1. Make a list of all the expenses that you would have if you owned a car. What would be the minimum cost to you each week? Is it worth it?
2. What do you know about insurance? Pick up some leaflets from your local insurance office. If you were married, with your own house and a car, what sort of insurances would you need?
3. What things should be checked regularly on a car?
4. If you were saving up to buy a car, where would you keep your money? Find out where your money would gain the greatest interest: the Trustee Savings Bank, the National Savings Bank (Post Office), an ordinary bank or a building society?

5. A car is only one of the big purchases where the buyer
   can be let down. Find out about your rights as a consumer. Can you normally get your money back on faulty
   goods? Are guarantees worth anything? Where is your
   nearest Consumer Advice Centre? You could invite one
   of the staff to tell you about their work.

A CALL FOR HELP

★

Characters

JO PACKER ⎱ *Samaritans*
LIZ HILL ⎰
TINA WILLIAMS
MARGARET WALKER, *A social worker*
MRS. FRASER, *Tina's neighbour*
POLICEMAN

*Note: This could be an all female play if you like,
if you make the policeman a policewoman*

A Call for Help

Scene I

The Samaritans' office

JO: (*Picks up phone.*) Hello. Samaritans here. Can I help you?

TINA: Hello.

JO: Hello. (*Pause.*) Hello. Who is that please? Can I help you?

TINA: Is that the Samaritans?

JO: Yes, this is the Samaritans. Please speak up. Can I help you? Have you got a problem?

TINA: Yes. I need your help.

JO: Please tell me your name.

TINA: Tina. Tina Williams.

JO: Tina. Where are you speaking from? (*Pause.*) Tina. Are you still there? Please speak up? What sort of help do you need? What is your problem? Where are you speaking from? . . . It looks as though she's hung up. Tina, are you there?

TINA: Yes. I'm still here. I'm in a call box. I'm speaking from a call box in Streatfield Avenue.

JO: Can you tell me the number of the telephone, so I can ring you back when the pips go?

TINA: I don't want to bother you only . . .

JO: Tina, that's what we're here for. You must tell me your number or I won't be able to help you.

TINA: It's Allenton 4142. Oh dear. There are the pips.

JO: Allenton 4142. O.K. Stay in the box. I'll ring you back . . . Sounds as if she's pretty desperate. I'll ring back now. What's the code for Allenton?

LIZ: Double eight.

JO: O.K. 8 – 8 – 4 – 1 – 4 2. It's ringing. I don't think she's going to answer. Perhaps she's changed her mind. I hope she. . . . Hello. Is that you Tina? Good. Yes. It's the Samaritans here. Now, what's your problem, Tina?

TINA: I don't know how to tell you, really. It's all such a muddle. It just gets worse and worse. I can't stand it any more.

JO: Yes I know. We're used to people's troubles here, Tina. Tell me how it all started. Just tell me slowly.

LIZ: Ask for her address. She might hang up on you.

JO: Now Tina, before you tell me what your problems are, can you tell me your address? You don't have to, if you don't want to, but it does mean that we can help you more if we know where you live.

TINA: It's 9 Gosport Terrace, Allenton. But I don't know if I'll be there much longer.

JO: Why is that, Tina? Are you going to move?

TINA: I'm behind with the rent. The landlord says I'll have to go if I don't pay up soon.

JO: That's not a problem, Tina. If you've got money troubles, the Social Security people will help you out.

TINA: That's just it. The rent isn't my real problem. It's just that I can't stand it any more. It's the baby. I'm afraid I might do something awful to him. He cries all night and all day. I can't get a wink of sleep. I'm scared that I'll belt him. I'm frightened. I really am.

JO: Can't your husband give you a hand with the baby?

TINA: Him? He did a bunk three months ago. I haven't seen him since.

JO: Who's looking after the baby now, Tina?

TINA: My mum's come over for the evening. She can't do much. She has to look after my dad. He's off work with his back. Besides, she can't stand the baby crying either.

JO: But you're not saying that you're worried because your baby cries, Tina? All babies cry.

TINA: Not all day and all night they don't. I get to the stage where I don't know what I'm doing any more. I did hit him once.

TINA: Now come on, Tina. You don't sound like a baby basher to me. You're obviously a very good mother and you love your baby. That's why you're so concerned about him.

TINA: But what can I do? I can't go on like this for much longer.

JO: Why don't you go and see your doctor? I'm sure he'll be able to help you. If you give me the name of your doctor, I'll give him a ring and tell him about your problems. He can arrange for someone from the Welfare to call who can give you a bit of help in the daytime.

TINA: But the baby's not poorly. He just cries a lot.

JO: I know, Tina. But all the same, you should take him to the doctor. And you might get sick yourself, if you don't see a doctor soon.

TINA: I'll think about it. All that waiting at the doctor's, and then what'll I tell him? He'll think I'm off my trolley.

JO: I'm sure he won't. Now what's your doctor's name?

TINA: Dr. Robertson in Copse Way.

JO: O.K. I'll give him a ring tomorrow. You go along to the surgery as soon as you can. Now, don't worry. Everything will be all right. You'll see.

TINA: Thanks. Thanks a lot. I feel a lot better, just talking to you. I'll think about what you say.

JO: Bye now, Tina, we'll be in touch.

(*Hangs up the phone.*)

LIZ: What was all that about then?

JO: It could be a false alarm. Or one of those things that solve themselves. But all the same, we can't take any chances. Baby bashing is a serious thing.

LIZ: Do you think it's as bad as all that?

JO: It might be. Baby bashers aren't really bad. They're just people that can't cope, that's all. I'll ring Dr. Robertson tomorrow morning, just to make sure. After all, someone should go along from the Welfare to see Tina Williams.

Scene II

Outside Tina's house. Next day.

(*Margaret knocks on Tina's Door. Waits. Knocks again.*)

MRS. FRASER: She ain't there.

MARGARET: You mean, Mrs. Williams has gone out?

MRS. FRASER: Went out an hour ago. Pushing the pram she was.

MARGARET: Do you know where she's gone?

MRS. FRASER: No. She never said nothing to me.

MARGARET: All right. I'll call again later. If she comes back, will you tell her that someone called from the Welfare.

MRS. FRASER: O.K., love, I'll do that. Hey, what's this? Police coming here. Well I never.

(*Policeman comes in.*)

POLICEMAN: Is this where Mrs. Williams lives?

MRS. FRASER: Yes it is, but she's gone out.

POLICEMAN: I know she's out. Poor thing is out in more ways than one.

MARGARET: What's the matter, constable? Is there anything wrong?

POLICEMAN: I'll say there's something wrong. Mrs. Williams has just been knocked down in the High Street. This is the only address we have for her.

MARGARET: What about the baby?

POLICEMAN: What baby? She was on her own.

MRS. FRASER: Maybe she left it outside a shop?

POLICEMAN: That's possible. I'll radio the station to check.

MARGARET: Maybe she left it at home? She could have come back and left it. Then remembered something she'd forgotten and popped out.

POLICEMAN: Could be. Perhaps we'd better break in and take a look.

MARGARET: I'll give you a hand. I'd better explain. I'm Margaret Walker from the Welfare. The Samaritans asked me to call on Mrs. Williams. She seems to have had a spot of trouble.

POLICEMAN: Well, we'd better look for this baby.

MRS. FRASER: That side window's open. You can get in there.

POLICEMAN: I'll climb in and then let you in, miss. You'll be better than me with abandoned babies.

(*Goes out.*)

MRS. FRASER: Sorry I can't help you. I've got a bad back you know. Funny thing. I can't hear any baby. And that baby howls all day and all night.

POLICEMAN: (*Comes in.*) No sign of a baby in there. Not even a pram. What about the husband?

MRS. FRASER: What husband? He went off and left her three months back. Never been sight nor sound of him since.

POLICEMAN: Well I'd better get back to the station. She must have left it outside a shop in the High Street. Probably found by now. We'll have to try and trace the parents. You said the Samaritans asked you to call?

MARGARET: That's right. You could give them a ring. They might know more about Tina. I'll have to be getting on with my calls. Could you ring my office and let me know when you find the baby?

POLICEMAN: I'll do that, miss. Cheerio.

Scene III

The Samaritans' office

LIZ: Hello Jo. Had a good day?

JO: I most certainly have not. You know the girl who rang up last night?

LIZ: Tina—I think you said her name was?

JO: That's the one. She was knocked down in the High Street this afternoon.

LIZ: Oh no! How awful! What about the baby?

JO: That's the problem. The baby's vanished. She wasn't pushing the pram at the time.

LIZ: Maybe she left it at home while she went shopping?

JO: The police broke into her house and the baby wasn't there. I asked a Welfare worker to go round and she told the police about Tina phoning us.

LIZ: So the police got in touch with you, did they?

JO: At work, too! I think the boss thought I was being arrested.

LIZ: But what about the baby? What can she have done with that?

JO: I don't know. She's still unconscious and the police are searching all over the place. They said they'd ring if they found it.

(*Phone rings.*)

LIZ: That may be them now.

JO: I doubt it. Probably a client. Hello. Samaritans here. Can I help you? Yes ... (*Pause.*) ... You what? Look, what's your address? Forty-one Townsend Road. And your name? Mrs. Ellison. All right Mrs. Ellison, someone will be along soon. Yes, we do know whose it is. You've done the right thing. (*Pause.*) Oh I see. Well I don't see that that matters now. It'll be a secret between you and me. Thank you Mrs. Ellison, we'll see you later.

LIZ: Who was that?

JO: Mrs. Ellison.

LIZ: But what has she done?

JO: She found a baby in a pram outside her house this afternoon. There was a note on the pram, telling whoever found it, to call the Samaritans.

LIZ: But it's six o'clock in the evening now.

JO: I know. She couldn't resist playing with it for a while. But now her husband's come back from work and he's made her phone us.

LIZ: So Tina's baby's found.

JO: Yes. All's well that ends well, I hope. I'll phone the police and tell them where to find the baby.

Scene IV

Hospital. A few days later.

JO: Hello there Tina. You haven't met me before, but we talked on the phone. I'm Jo from the Samaritans.

TINA: Hello. Margaret's told me all about you.

JO: How are you feeling now?

TINA: I'm fine thanks, I was lucky to get away with a bang on the head and a broken leg.

MARGARET: And the hospital is looking after the baby.

JO: That's what I can't understand, Tina. Why did you abandon the baby? I thought you were feeling better after talking to us.

TINA: So I was. Then that afternoon there was a man who came to the door with a Court Order to evict me. Well suddenly I just couldn't cope any more. The baby was crying. There was no money left for food or anything. So I wrote the note and left the baby outside someone's house. There was a swing in the garden, so I thought they must have kids. After that I don't remember anything at all, until I woke up here.

MARGARET: I've found a place for the baby at a day nursery. Once you're up and about again, I think you should try to get a part-time job. It's not what I recommend usually for young mothers, but I think you've been cooped up in that flat too long. You need to get out a bit and meet people again.

TINA: That would be lovely.

JO: The Social Security people are working on the rent arrears. Why didn't you tell us that your husband wasn't paying any maintenance?

MARGARET: What have you been living on?

TINA: My mum's let me have a bit now and again. I didn't like to ask for money from the Social Security. I mean, that's begging isn't it? My mum says you mustn't get money from them because they'll put spies on you to make sure you're not living with men.

MARGARET: Don't   you   believe   all   you   read   in   the newspapers. It's what you're entitled to. We'll get you all the arrears of benefit as well.

TINA: You know, I've been thinking. We called the baby Arthur after his father. But I think I'll change his name to Sam.

JO: Why Sam?

TINA: After the Samaritans, of course. They've been more help to me than his father ever was!

A CALL FOR HELP

Points to Discuss

1. Why do you think that the Samaritans' job is essential?
2. Why do people want to commit suicide?
3. What other situations would people phone the Samaritans about?
4. What sort of people do you think work for the Samaritans? Are they paid? Are they trained?
5. Think of reasons why someone in desperate trouble might prefer to talk to a stranger rather than to family or friends.

Things to Do

1. One thing *not* to do is to telephone the Samaritans, unless you really need help. But you could find out the number of your local branch and where it is. One of the members may be willing to come and talk to you.
2. What other organisations staffed by volunteers are there in your area to help people? Who do they help?
3. Here is a list of emergencies. What would you do, and who would you phone?
   (*a*) A child swallows pills by accident.
   (*b*) You're first on the scene at a car crash and a car is on fire.
   (*c*) You see a suspicious character lurking round the house next door.
   (*d*) You're given the sack at work for something you haven't done.
   (*e*) Your wife/husband doesn't come home one night.
   (*f*) An old lady collapses in front of you in the street.